The Story of a Special Day
Volume 195

July
13

The 194th day of the year (195th in leap years).
There are 171 days remaining until the end of the year.

by Michael Dobson

Timespinner
Press

This book is also available in e-book form for Kindle, e-pub devices, and other formats from your favorite online booksellers.

For more information about the series, about us, or about your special day, please email us at editor@timespinnerpress.com.

Look for other volumes in *The Story of a Special Day*, coming often. See www.timespinnerpress.com for details and for the most recent information.

Table of Contents

For the definition of "O.S.," "CE," and "BCE" used with some dates , see the section "On Names and Dates."

Quote of the Day

"It's one world, pal. We're all neighbors."

Frank Sinatra, singer
(December 12, 1915 — May 14, 1998)
First recording session, July 13, 1939

Today in History

July 13

Frank Sinatra (1943)

Event of the Day
Frank Sinatra's First Recording

On July 13, 1939, 23-year old singer Frank Sinatra went into the recording studio with the Harry James Orchestra to cut the first of many records that would make up his legendary musical career. His first release from that session, "From the Bottom of My Heart," sold about 8,000 copies, and the other singles didn't do much better. (They're collected on the 1995 reissue *Harry James and His Orchestra (featuring Frank Sinatra*, with alternate takes and live performances added in.)

Frank Sinatra started singing professionally while still a teenager. With his group, the Hoboken Four, Sinatra won first prize on Major Bowes Amateur Hour (the American Idol of its day), earning a six-month nationwide concert tour. He worked as a singing waiter until he was discovered by bandleader Harry James. He moved from Harry James to Tommy Dorsey before going solo in 1941.

By the following year, he was a phenomenon. It was "Sinatramania," the passion of bobby-soxers (teenage women). When 35,000 fans showed up for a concert that could only take 250, a near riot broke out.

Sinatra's career went through numerous stages. After the end of "Sinatramania," Frank and his Rat Pack friends dominated Las Vegas entertainment. He began a film career, winning an Academy Award as Best Supporting Actor for From Here to Eternity.

His albums for Capitol, beginning with *Songs for Young Lovers*, in collaboration with Nelson Riddle, established a new creative chapter. He formed his own record label, Reprise, which became an industry powerhouse. He was involved with politics, and rumors continue to associate him with underworld figures.

By any measure, Frank Sinatra was a towering figure in popular music. Called "the greatest singer of the 20th century," he was awarded eleven Grammys, including a lifetime achievement award and a legend award, the Presidential Medal of Freedom, the Congressional Gold Medal, and Kennedy Center Honors.

Frank Sinatra (1955)

New York City draft riots

What Happened on July 13?

From the creation of great works of engineering and art, to devastating wars and natural disasters, thousands of years of history have left their mark on each and every day of the year. Here are some important events that occurred on July 13. (Items with a photo or illustration are boxed.)

1787 — The Confederation Congress (under the Articles of Confederation that preceded the Constitution) passes the **Northwest Ordinance**, creating the Northwest Territory (states surrounding the Great Lakes, from Ohio into Minnesota). It was one of the most significant acts of the Confederation, establishing for the first time a process for admitting new states to the union.

1863 — The **New York City draft riots**, in response to a Congressional draft of men to fight in the American Civil War, breaks out, resulting in three days violent disturbances throughout the city, developing into a race riot, with working class whites attacking black neighborhoods until sufficient military forces could reach the city. The official death toll exceeded 100.

1919 — The British **airship R34** returns to England after **successfully crossing the Atlantic** in both directions, carrying a crew of 26, plus a stowaway and a cat. This was the third successful crossing of the Atlantic Ocean by air and the first round-trip. Charles Lindbergh's nonstop New York to Paris flight would not happen for another eight years.

1973 — **Watergate: Nixon Tapes Revealed**. In response to questions from the Senate Special Committee investigating the Watergate break-in, White House aide Alexander Butterfield reveals the existence of the White House recording system.

1977 — A **New York City electrical blackout** shuts down the city for over eight hours, with widespread looting and vandalism. This particular blackout has been used or mentioned in a variety of films, books, and tv series, including the film *Men in Black*, Jackie Collins' novel *Chances*, and the tv series *The Get Down*.

1985 — For the duration of a minor surgical procedure on US President Ronald Reagan, Vice President George H. W. Bush becomes the **first Acting President of the United States under the 25th Amendment** to the Constitution.

A gasoline advertisement featuring the airship R34/

Quote of the Day

"The Force is within you. Force yourself."

Harrison Ford, actor
born July 13, 1942

Births
and
Deaths

THE AC-
MAGNA

July 13

General Leslie Groves, commander of the Manhattan Project (right), with J. Robert Oppenheimer, scientific director, at Ground Zero of the Trinity nuclear weapon test (1945). Leslie Groves died July 13, 1970.

Notable July 13 People

With the current world population at about seven billion people, on average about 19 million people also celebrate their birthdays on July 13 — and that isn't counting millions and millions who came before! No matter when you were born, you share your birthday with many special people whose accomplishments (and occasionally embarrassments) have been noted as part of history.

In this section, you'll meet fascinating people who share your birthday. They're organized by what they're famous for, and then in reverse chronological order from most recent to earliest. Those who are shown in photographs or artwork have a box around them. We don't have photos of everyone, so please forgive us if your favorite person is missing.

Some of these people you've heard of, others will be new to you, but they all make up an important part of the reason that July 13 is a truly special day!

"An Artist's Studio," by Thomas Rowlandson (1814)

Who Was Born on July 13?

Art and Illustration

Thomas Rowlandson, English illustrator known for his caricatures. *(1756)*

Business and Food

Paul Prudhomme, celebrity chef specializing in Creole and Cajun cuisines. *(1940)*

Kaoru Ishikawa (石川 馨), Japanese management theorist important in the development of formal quality systems in Japanese manufacturing, also known for his cause-and-effect diagram known as the *Ishikawa diagram* or the *fishbone diagram*. *(1915)*

John Jacob Astor IV, prominent businessman and member of the Astor family, one of the world's richest men, went down on the RMS *Titanic* in 1912. *(1864)*

Military and Politics

Jack Kemp, professional football player who entered politics, serving nine terms in Congress and as Secretary of Housing and Urban Development under President George H. W. Bush. *(1935)*

Nathan Bedford Forrest, Confederate calvary general known as "the wizard of the saddle," later first Grand Wizard of the Ku Klux Klan. *(1821)*

Music

Rhonda Vincent, bluegrass singer and multi-instrumentalist known as "the new Queen of Bluegrass." *(1962)*

Louise Mandrell, country singer, sister of Barbara Mandrell. *(1954)*

Roger McGuinn, musician known as the lead singer and lead guitarist for The Byrds, member of the Rock and Roll Hall of Fame. *(1942)*

Performing Arts and Broadcasting

Ken Jeong, actor best known for the TV series *Community. (1969)*

Tom Kenny, animation voice artist best known as the voice of the title character on *SpongeBob SquarePants. (1962)*

Cameron Crowe, actor and screenwriter best known for his films *Fast Times at Ridgemont High, Jerry Maguire,* and *Almost Famous.* (1957)

Didi Conn, actress best known as "Frenchy" from the 1978 film *Grease. (1951)*

Nathan Bedford Forrest

Harrison Ford, in costume as "Indiana Jones" (2007)
(Photo: John Griffiths, CC BY-SA 2.0)

Cheech Marin, comedian best known as half of the comedy act Cheech & Chong. *(1946)*

Harrison Ford, actor who gained fame as Han Solo in the original *Star Wars* trilogy, named number one in *Empire's* "The Top 100 Movie Stars of All Time" list in 1997. *(1942)*

Patrick Stewart, actor best known for his roles as Jean-Luc Picard on *Star Trek: The Next Generation*, and as Professor Xavier in the *X-Men* film franchise. *(1940)*

Peter Gzowski, influential radio broadcaster known as "Mr. Canada." *(1934)*

Bob Crane, actor, musician, and radio personality best known for the title role in the sitcom *Hogan's Heroes*. *(1928)*

Robert H. Justman, television producer best known for *Star Trek*. *(1926)*

Benny Carle, pioneering children's television show host in Alabama, hosting over 400,000 children on his shows from the late 1940s through 1965. *(1926)*

Johnny Gilbert, game show announcer best known for *Jeopardy!* *(1923)*

Dave Garroway, founding host and anchor of *The Today Show* (NBC). *(1913)*

Kay Linaker-Phillips, B-movie actress and screenwriter of the 1958 cult film *The Blob*. *(1913)*

Science and Invention

Ernő Rubik, Hungarian inventor best known as the inventor of the mechanical puzzle Rubik's Cube. *(1944)*

Rubik's Cube (Photo: Fabio Fosso, CC BY-SA 2.0)

Sports

Michael Spinks, two-weight world champion boxer, Olympic gold medalist, member of the International Boxing Hall of Fame, brother of boxer Leon Spinks. *(1956)*

David Thompson, basketball player with the Denver Nuggets, Seattle SuperSonics, and NC State, member of the Basketball Hall of Fame and the College Basketball Hall of Fame. *(1954)*

Michael Spinks

Frank Ramsey, basketball player with the Boston Celtics and head coach of the Kentucky Colonels, inducted into the Basketball Hall of Fame and the College Basketball Hall of Fame. *(1931)*

Sven Davidson, Swedish tennis player inducted into the International Tennis Hall of Fame in 2007. *(1928)*

Writing and History

Ian Hislop, British satirist best known as editor of *Private Eye* and for his role on the BBC quiz show *Have I Got News For You*. *(1960)*

Wole Soyinka, Nigerian playwright and poet, first African to receive the Nobel Prize in Literature. *(1934)*

George Weller, Pulitzer Prize-winning war correspondent who claims to have been the first outside observer to reach Nagasaki after the atomic bombing in 1945. His reports were initially censored, but were eventually published in 2006 as *First Into Nagasaki*. *(1907)*

Kenneth Clark, British historian, museum director, and author best known as the producer and presenter of the BBC television series *Civilisation*. *(1903)*

Margaret Murray, archaeologist and folklorist known for her contributions to Egyptology and for her theories about early witch cults, involved in the early development of feminism. *(1863)*

Margaret Murray (1928)

Alfred Stieglitz in 1886 (self-portrait)

Who Died on July 13?

Art and Photography

Frida Kahlo, Mexican surrealist painter, husband of artist Diego Rivera. *(1954)*

Walt Kuhn, American painter who organized the famous Armory Show of 1913, which introduced America to modern European art. *(1949)*

Alfred Stieglitz, helped make photography an accepted art form, husband of painter Georgia O'Keefe. *(1946)*

Government and Military

Joachim Peiper, SS colonel, led the German advance in the Battle of the Bulge (Operation Wacht am Rhein), in command of the forces who committed the Malmedy Massacre of US prisoners of war. (He is a character in my 2003 novel *Fox at the Front.*) *(1976)*

Leslie Groves, US general who built the Pentagon and managed the Manhattan Project to build the first nuclear bomb. *(1970)* *(Photo pg. 12)*

They-Fear-Even-His-Horses (Tȟašúŋke Kȟokípȟapi), Oglala Sioux chief who participated in Red Cloud's War. His name is sometimes translated as Young-Man-Afraid-of-His-Horses, but the above translation is more accurate. *(1893)*

John C. Frémont, noted explorer, territorial governor of Arizona, Senator from California, first Presidential candidate of the newly-formed anti-slavery Republican Party. *(1890)*

Jean-Paul Marat, Jacobin journalist and politician considered a martyr of the French Revolution because he was assassinated by Girondist sympathizer Charlotte Corday in his bath. The Marquis de Sade gave the eulogy at his funeral. The 1963 Broadway hit *Marat/Sade* centers around his assassination. *(1793)*

Letters

Nadine Gordimer, South African anti-apartheid writer who received the 1991 Nobel Prize in Literature *(2006)*

Music

Red Buttons, American comedian and actor who won an Academy Award for Best Supporting Actor for the 1957 film *Sayonara. (2006)*

Arthur Schoenberg, modern composer known for developing the twelve-tone technique. *(1951)*

"The Death of Marat," Jacques-Louis David

Performing Arts

Cory Monteith, actor and musician best known for playing Finn Hudson on the television series *Glee*. *(2013)*

Pandro S. Berman, RKO film producer who oversaw the Fred Astaire/Ginger Rogers musicals and many other classic films. *(1951)*

Science and Education

Patrick Blackett, English experimental physicist who won the Nobel Prize in Physics for 1948 for work on cosmic radiation. *(1974)*

Mary E. Byrd, pioneering science educator who helped promote co-education in America. *(1934)*

Gabriel Lippmann, received the Nobel Prize in Physics in 1908 for his work on reproducing colors photographically. *(1921)*

James Bradley, served as the Astronomer Royal of Great Britain, made fundamental discoveries in astronomy. *(1762)*

Sports

George Steinbrenner, principal owner and managing partner of the New York Yankees for nearly four decades. *(1951)*

George Steinbrenner

Quote of the Day

"Football is democratic, capitalism, whereas soccer is a European socialist sport."

Jack Kemp, politician and football player
born July 13, 1935

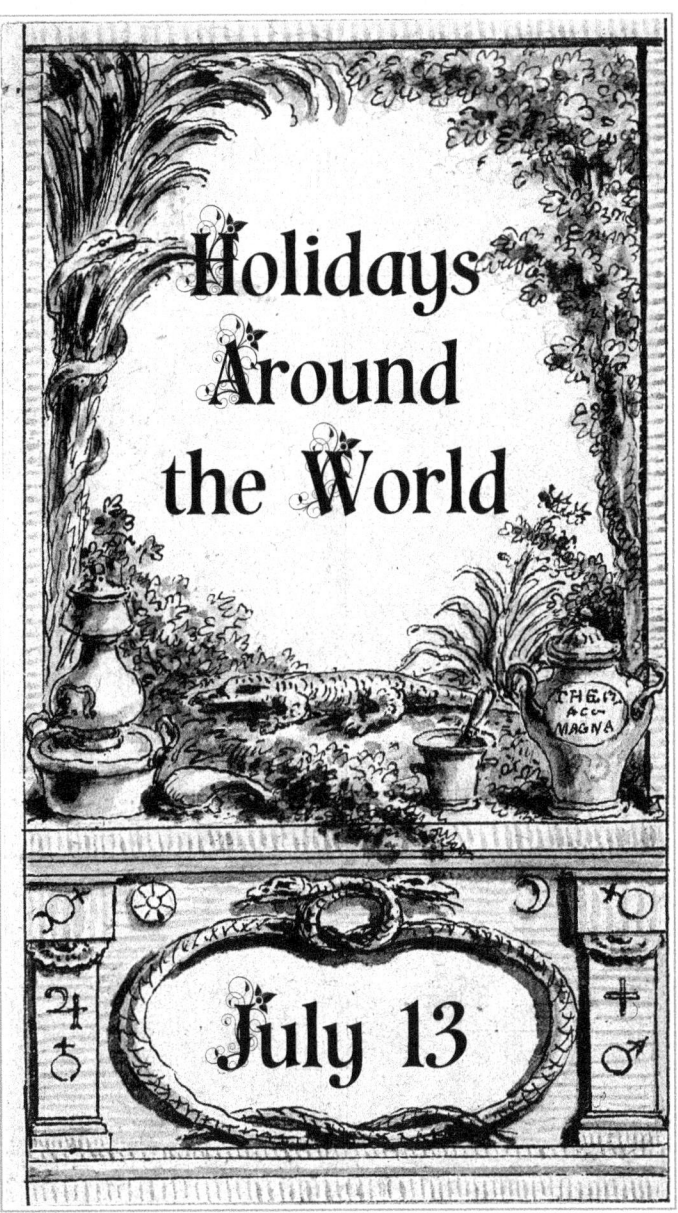

Holidays
Around
the World

July 13

31

Friday the Thirteenth (Photo: W. J. Pilsak, CC BY-SA 3.0)

Holidays Around the World

If you're looking for a reason to take your special day off, you should know that every single day is a holiday somewhere in the world! Here's some of what you can celebrate on July 13!

Friday the Thirteenth

While June 13 doesn't come on Friday every year (see "What Day of the Week is June 13"), sooner or later, every 13th day of the month eventually lands on the last day of the week.

Friday the 13th is considered an unlucky day in many (but not all) Western nations. Both the number 13 and Friday have a history of being thought unlucky, so when you put the two together, some people begin to worry. The idea that Friday is unlucky seems to be a maritime superstition — sailors believed it was unlucky to start a voyage on a Friday.

As far as the number 13 goes, there are a number of theories.One theory is that it refers to the 13 people around the table at the Last Supper, one of whom (Judas) would shortly betray Jesus. Others point out that on Friday, October 13, 1307, the Knights Templar were arrested, and many of them were later tortured and killed.

Fear of the number thirteen is common enough that a psychological condition, *triskaidekaphobia*, is named for it! (Fear of Friday the 13th in particular is known as *paraskevidekatriaphobi*a.) According to some researchers, between 17 and 21 million people in the US alone are bothered by Friday the 13th. Fear of thirteen is so common that many tall buildings skip 13 when numbering floors.

In Spanish-speaking countries, as well as in Greece, they worry about Tuesday the 13th (*martes trece*) instead — though either way, June 13 qualifies. In Italy, though, 13 is a lucky number — but watch out for Friday the 17th!

General Events

Inventor's Day (Hungary)

A number of nations set aside a special day each year to recognize the contribution of inventors.

Hungarian Inventor's Day (*Magyar feltalálók napja*) is sponsored by the Association of Hungarian Inventors and is celebrated on June 13 in honor of Nobel Prize-winning physiologist Albert Szent-Györgyi, who patented his method of synthesizing Vitamin C on this day in 1941. (*Always June 13*)

Statehood Day (Montenegro)

The Balkan nation of Montenegro celebrates Statehood Day to commemorate the recognition of Montenegran sovereignty by the Berlin Congress on July 13, 1878. (*Always June 13*)

Trooping the Colour (The Queen's Official Birthday Parade)

Although the birthday of HM Queen Elizabeth II of England is actually April 21, 1926, the Queen's Official Birthday falls on different days, depending on the year. A spectacular military parade, called Trooping the Colour, involving nearly 1,000 men, 200 horses, six bands, and the Royal Family, begins at Buckingham Palace.

(*Any date between June 11 and June 17, varies by year*)

Princess (later Queen) Elizabeth at a Trooping of the Colour
ceremony for her father George VI (1951)

Food Holidays

In the United States, almost every day of the year is dedicated to a particular food. (Some other countries do this also, but not every day.) Sponsored by manufacturers, retailers, farmers, or simply fans, these days are often proclaimed by the President, Congress, state governors, or mayors. Given that there are more different foods than days of the year, some days honor more than one kind of food!

July 13 is **National Cheese Pizza Day.** According to Foodimentary.com, over 93% of Americans eat at least one pizza a month! Other sources claim July 13 is **National French Fries Day** or **National BBQ Day**, so have some of each while you're still hungry.

In addition, the entire month of July is used to celebrate numerous foods. Here's a list of what to eat in the month of July!

- Dairy Month
- Georgia Blueberry Month
- National Baked Beans Month
- National Candy Month
- National Fruit and Veggies Month
- National Hot Dog Month
- National Ice Cream Month
- National Picnic Month
- National Rosé Wine Month

Christian Feast Days and Holidays

Feast of St. Anthony (Boston and Brazil)

Saint Anthony of Padua's feast day of July 13 gets special celebration in at least two places. In Boston's North End, a group of Italians originally from Montefalcione honor their patron saint with public decorations and a great feast. St. Anthony is also the patron saint of Brazil, and because his feast day is the day before Brazilian Valentine's Day, he's also acquired a reputation as a matchmaker. *(Photo pg. 38)*

Saint Feast Days

Each day in the year is considered a feast day for one or more saints. They are somewhat different in western Christianity (Catholicism and many forms of Protestantism) and in eastern (Orthodox) Christianity. There are many others; this is a selection.

In *Western Christianity*, it is the feast day of Saints Abd-al-Masih, Abel of Tacla Haimonot (Coptic), Clelia Barbieri, Conrad Weiser (Episcopal), Eugenius of Carthage, Holy Roman Emperor Henry II, Teresa of the Andes, and Silas

In *Eastern Orthodox Christianity*, it is also the commemoration of the Synaxis of the Holy Archangel Gabriel, Venerable Steven the Sabaite, and Saint Julian of Cenomanis. (These are observed on July 26 by "Old Calendarists.")

S. ANTONIVS DE PADVA.

Saint Anthony of Padua

Honorary Months

Presidents, Congresses, and nations around the world issue proclamations recognizing particular months to honor certain causes. These events generally fall in July, though honorary months do come and go. Holidays established by states and nonprofit organizations are listed if verified. If not otherwise specified, all months are US. There is some variation from year to year; some celebratory months get added and others get dropped. Two places to get up to date information are the current edition of *Chase's Calendar of Events* or the website Brownielocks (www.brownielocks.com). Here are some honorary designations for July.

- Adopt-a-Cat Month
- African-American Music Appreciation Month
- Caribbean-American Heritage Month
- Child Vision Awareness Month
- Fireworks Safety Month
- International Surf Music Month
- National Camping Month
- National LGBT Pride Month
- National Smile Month
- National Zoo and Aquarium Month
- PTSD Awareness Month

Moveable and Multi-Day Events

Some events take place over a specific week or time period. Start and finish dates may vary from year to year. Some events occur on different days each year (such as "fourth Saturday of a month"). These events sometimes take place on July 13.

Week that has July 13 in it
- National Automobile Service Professionals Week

Week containing National Flag Day (July 14)
- National Flag Week (US)

Second Saturday in July
- International Young Eagles Day
- Missing Mutts Awareness Day
- World Bike Naked Day

Second Sunday in July
- Abused Women and Children's Awareness Day
- Children's Sunday
- Multicultural American Child Day
- Race Unity Day

Just for Fun

Anybody can make up a holiday, and many people do! While none of these are officially recognized and some may come and go, here are a few more holidays for June 13.

- Blame Someone Else Day
- Kitchen Klutzes of America Day
- Sewing Machine Day
- Weed Your Garden Day

Poster for the 140th National Flag Day, 1917

Quote of the Day

"We have the power to transform the quality of our lives."

Werner Erhard, founder of est
born September 5, 1935

About
the
Month
of

July

July, from the *Brevarium Grimani* by Simon Bening (c.1510)

July: The Seventh Month

"Here men from the planet Earth first set foot upon the Moon. July 1969 AD.""

— Plaque left on the site of the Apollo 11 landing.

In the original Roman calendar, the month of July was named *Quintilis*, the fifth month, because the Romans originally counted the first of March as the beginning of the new year.

Quintilis was renamed July by the Roman senate in honor of Gaius Julius Caesar after his death in 44 BCE, because Caesar, among his other accomplishments, had undertaken a major calendar reform, known as the Julian calendar, which remained the standard European calendar until 1582 CE. (Not to be outdone, Emperor Augustus arranged for the next month, Sextilis, to be renamed in his honor.)

July is one of the seven months with 31 days. In a common (non-leap) year, it always starts on the same day of the week as April, and on the same day of the week as January in leap years. Strangely, in common years, no other month of the year ends on the same day of the week as July! (In leap years, the last day of July and January fall on the same day.)

July in Other Cultures

In Latin, the month of July was spelled *Iulius*, as the Romans did not have the letter "J."

In Albanian, the month is *korrik*. Arabs call the month يوليه (*yūlia*).

It is юли (*juli*) in Bulgaria, *lipanj* in Croatia, and *červen* in Czech.

The Finns call the month *kesäkuu* and the Greeks call it Ιούλιος (*Ioúlios*).

The Hebrew calendar has different months, but when they refer to the Gregorian month, it's יולי (*yûlî*).

In Gaelic, July is *Meitheamh mi an Mheitheamh*, and in Russian, it is июнь (*ijun'*).

The Chinese use 六月 (*liùyuè* in Mandarin); Koreans 유월 (*yuweol*); and it's 腑軷 (*tháng sáu*) in Vietnamese.

July Sayings and Superstitions

Farming

- The corn harvest will be good if the corn growing in the fields is "knee high by the Fourth of July."
- "If the first of July be rainy weather, 'twill rain more or less for four weeks together."
- "Rain or dry, plant your turnips on the Fourth of July."

Marriage

- "Those who in July do wed, must labor for their daily bread."

As for which day of the week, that's easy.

Monday for health, Tuesday for wealth,
Wednesday best of all, Thursday for losses,
Friday for crosses, Saturday for no luck at all.

July Symbols

Birthstone: Ruby (symbolizes success, devotion, and integrity.)

Ruby

Birth Flowers: Water Lily (purity of heart) or Larkspur (lightness and levity.)

Water Lily (Photo: Dinkum)

Birth Tree: Elm (strength of will and intuition)

"Study of an Elm Tree," John Constable (1821)

July, by Eugène Grasset

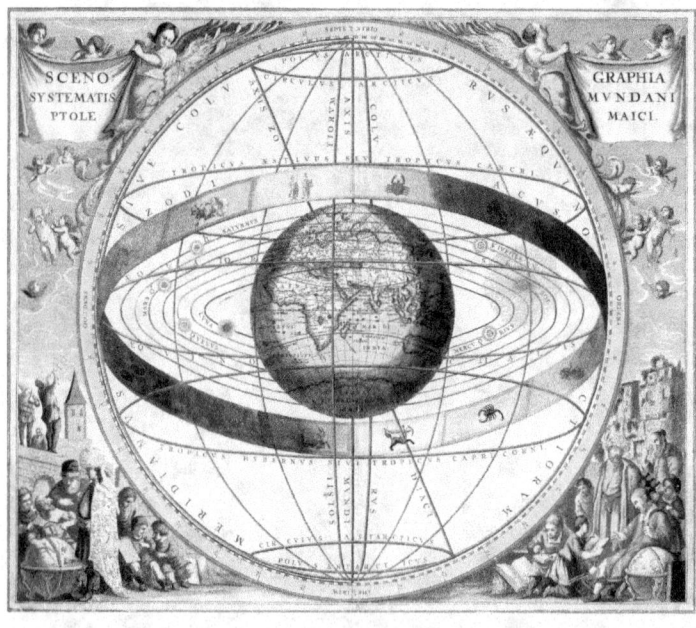

Scenography of the Ptolemaic Cosmography, by Johannes van Loon, based on Andreas Cellarius's *Harmonia Macrocosmica,* 1660

July 13 Zodiac Signs

From the perspective of someone on Earth, the Sun appears to move through the sky throughout the year, along a path astronomers call the *ecliptic plane*. The ecliptic plane is divided into twelve constellations, known as the zodiac, based on traditionally observed patterns of stars. On your birthday, you can't see your constellation, because it's in the daytime sky.

The zodiac was first developed by Babylonian astronomers about 2,500 years ago. Because they were unaware that the Earth wobbles like a spinning top (known as *precession*), they didn't make allowance for the fact that the Sun's path through the zodiac changes over time.

That means there are now two sets of dates for your birth sign. The *tropical dates* are the original Babylonian dates; the *sidereal dates* tell you where the Sun actually appears as it moves along its annual path.

For July 13, the tropical signs is **Cancer** and the sidereal sign is **Gemini**.

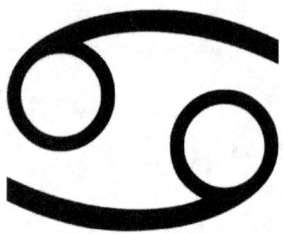

Cancer

Tropical June 21 to July 22
Sidereal July 16 to August 15

The Greek word for "crab" is Καρκινος (Karkinos), later Latinized as carcinus, which evolved into our word cancer. In Greek mythology. In one telling, when Hercules was battling the Hydra, Zeus's wife Hera sent Karkinos to distract the hero, but Hercules kicked it with such force that it was thrown into the sky, becoming a constellation. (Some say that Hercules crushed the crab with his foot and that Hera placed the crab in the night sky as a reward for its service.)

Because of the association with the disease, some astrologers refer to those born under the sign of Cancer as "moon children," because the ruling planet of Cancer is the Moon.

Cancers (or Moon Children) are supposed to be loyal, dependable, caring, and adaptable, but can also be moody, self-pitying, and oversensitive. Cancers are supposed to be particularly compatible with Scorpios, Piceans, and other Cancers.

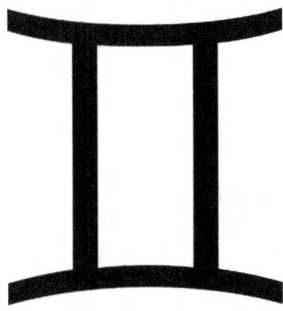

Gemini

Tropical May 22 to June 21
Sidereal June 16 to July 15

In Greek and Roman mythology, Castor and Pollux were twin brothers, both born to Leda. Castor, however, was a mortal, son of the King of Sparta, whereas Pollux was the son of Zeus, who had seduced (or raped) Leda while disguised as a swan. When Castor was killed, Pollux asked to share his divine immortality with his brother, and so Zeus transformed them both into the constellation of Gemini.

In astrology, Gemini is considered a masculine and air sign, ruled by Mercury. Geminis are supposed to be flexible, responsive, and sociable. Positive traits include intelligence and independence; negative traits include impatience and impulsiveness. Geminis are supposed to be particularly compatible with Aquarians, Libras, and other Geminis.

Illustration by Edward Penfield

What Day of the Week is July 13?

On what day of the week does July 13 fall?

Surprisingly, this isn't an easy question. Because the calendar year is 365 days long (366 in leap years), it doesn't divide evenly by the seven days of the week.

Also, the Earth goes around the Sun in about 365-1/4 days, so a calendar tends to drift over time. That's why the same date falls on different weekdays in different years.

This is made even more complicated by a change in calendars that took place in 1582. Our modern calendar has its roots in ancient Rome, in a calendar reform conducted by Julius Caesar. Caesar commissioned mathematicians to attack the problem, and they came up with the idea of leap years, and thus standardized the calendar for centuries to come. This was called the Julian calendar.

Over time, however, the small errors in Caesar's calculation compounded. That's why Pope Gregory XIII commissioned the Gregorian calendar, used in most of the world today. Some countries converted in 1582, when the calendar was first developed; some converted later; other still haven't changed.

Gregorian and Julian aren't the only types of calendars. The Hebrew year, the Islamic year, and many other calendars are used in different parts of the world and among different people.

You can convert Gregorian dates to other calendars, including the Hebrew calendar, the Islamic calendar, and even the Mayan calendar by visiting the Fourmilab Calendar Converter at http://www.fourmilab.ch/documents/calendar/.

Chinese calendar systems are quite complex and have changed several times; a full discussion is far beyond the scope of this book. If you're interested, you can find information here: http://www.hermetic.ch/cal_stud/chinese_cal.htm.

On Names and Dates

Historians use "CE" (Common Era) and "BCE" (Before the Common Era) instead of the more common "AD" (Anno Domini, or Year of Our Lord) and "BC" (Before Christ), reflecting the fact that the year-numbering system established by the Gregorian calendar is used throughout the world in many countries not culturally Christian.

The CE/BCE designation dates back to at least 1708, and has been adopted as a standard by the United Nations and the Universal Postal Union. Because this series of books covers events and people of all nations and cultures, we use the CE/BCE terms.

The abbreviation "O.S." ("Old Style") on some dates refers to the fact that the Russian Empire did not switch from the Julian to the Gregorian calendar at the same time as the rest of Europe, and therefore some figures and events have two dates.

Also, in the Julian calendar in England in the 16th century, the year began on March 25 rather than January 1. To avoid confusion with Gregorian dates, dates between January and March were often written using both years.

People and events whose original names are not in the Western alphabet have their native names (where possible) in the appropriate script shown in parenthesis. If you are using an e-reader to access an electronic version of this book, all characters don't always display on all devices.

A 50-year brass perpetual calendar.

Quote of the Day

"Time is an illusion, lunchtime doubly so."

Douglas Adams,
from *The Hitchhiker's Guide to the Galaxy*

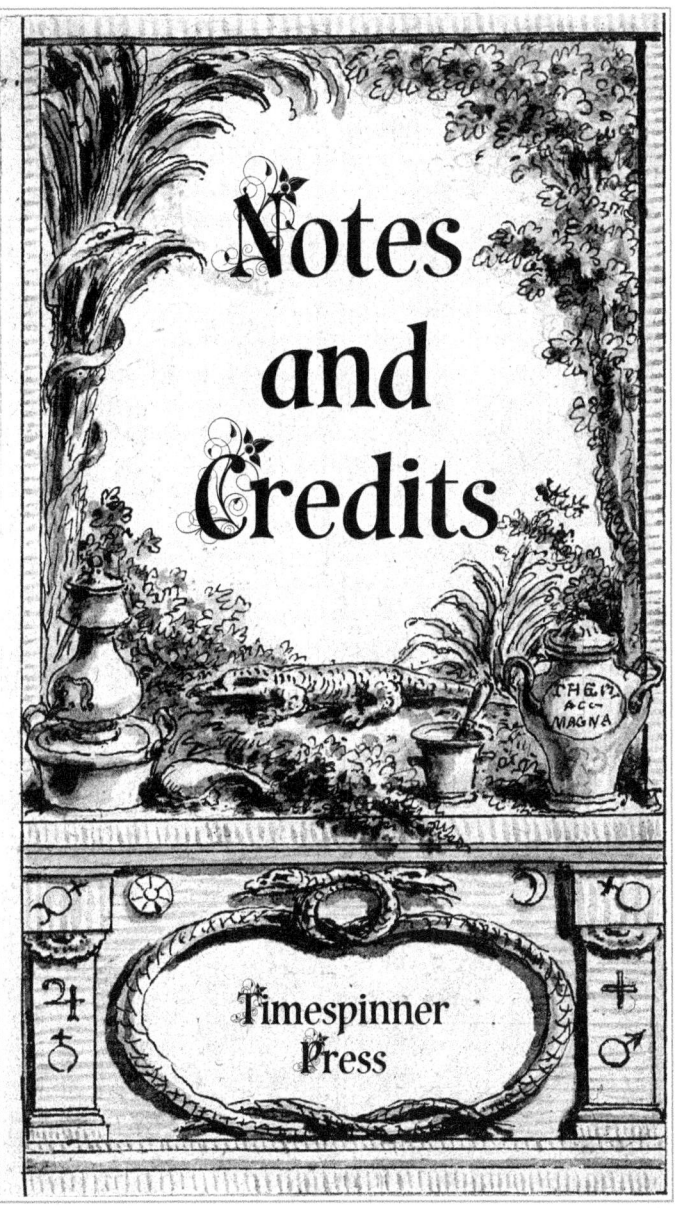

Notes
and
Credits

Timespinner
Press

Cartoon by John T. McCutcheon

Copyright, Credit, and Contact

Follow Us

Our blog "This Day in History" (http://timespinnerpress.com/this-day-in-history/) features short articles on events and people associated with each day, and updates several times each week. Also subscribe to the "Quote of the Day" at http://timespinnerpress.com/quote-of-the-day/. You can get daily links by following us on Facebook at TimespinnerPress, or on Twitter as @sidewisethinker.

Contact Us

Find an error or a format problem? Want information about the series, about us, or about when the volume for your special day might be available? Please email us at editor@timespinnerpress.com. (We also take requests if your special day isn't yet complete. Please give us at least six weeks' notice if possible.)

Sources

We owe a great debt to Wikipedia, which is our first stop for research. We attempt to make independent confirmation of all important dates and facts through a variety of other sources.

Other sources we frequently use include the Library of Congress; "on this day" listings from *Encyclopedia Britannica*, the *New York Times*, and the BBC; Omniglot for the names of months in other languages; *Chase's Calendar of Events;* and, of course, the always essential Google.

All art and photographs are either in the public domain, used under a Creative Commons license, or with a "fair use" justification, and most frequently come from Wikimedia Commons and the Library of Congress Prints and Photographs Division.

Attribution is provided where possible, or as requested by the copyright owner, or when there is particular historical significance, listed below. For information about any particular illustration or photograph, please contact us.

Credits

1. The 1947 cover photograph of Frank Sinatra at Liederkranz Hall, New York, was taken by William P. Gottlieb, and is part of the William P. Gottlieb Collection at the Library of Congress. In accordance with the wishes of William Gottlieb, the photographs in this collection entered into the public domain on February 16, 2010.

2. The illustration of the month of July used on the back cover is from the French Gothic illuminated manuscript *Les Très Riches Heures du duc de Berry* by the Limbourg Brothers, Jean Colombe, and an intermediate painter whose name is lost to history. It is in the public domain because its copyright has expired.

3. The box graphic used on the first page is from a 1916 pamphlet entitled "Divorce versus Democracy" authored by G. K. Chesterton, originally published in London by the Society of St. Peter and St. Paul. It is in the public domain in the US because it was published prior to 1923, and is in the public domain in all countries (including the country of origin) in which the copyright time is the author's life plus 70 years or less.

4. The graphic design for the section pages in this book is from a design originally created for a pharmacy label. It is courtesy of Wellcome Images (ICV No 11073, photo V0010813), and is used here under CC BY-SA 4.0.

5. The 1943 photo of Frank Sinatra appeared in an advertisement in *Billboard* magazine. It is in the public domain because it was first published in the United States between 1923 and 1977 without a copyright notice.

6. The publicity photograph of Frank Sinatra from a 1955 television production of *Our Town* is in the public domain because it was first published in the United States between 1923 and 1977 without a copyright notice. Typically, publicity photographs are not copyrighted because of the way in which they are intended to be used.

7. The drawing of rioters during the 1863 New York Draft Riot originally appeared in William J. Bradley's *The Civil War: Fort Sumter to Appomattox*. It is in the public domain because it was first published prior to 1923 and its copyright has expired.

8. The advertisement for Socony gasoline appeared in the July 15, 1919, issue of the New York *Sun*. It is in the public domain because it was first published in the United States between 1923 and 1977 without a copyright notice.

9. The 1945 US Army Corps of Engineers photograph of J. Robert Oppenheimer and Leslie Groves is in the public domain as a work created by a soldier or civilian employee of the US Army as part of that person's official duties.

10. The 1814 watercolor "An Artist's Studio" by Thomas Rowlandson is in the public domain because its copyright has expired. The file is courtesy Google Art Project.

11. The 19th century photograph of Confederate General Nathan Bedford Forest is in the public domain because its copyright has expired.

12. The 2007 photograph of Harrison Ford in costume as "Indiana Jones" was taken by John Griffiths, and is used here under CC BY-SA 2.0.

13. The 2008 photograph of a Rubik's Cube was taken by Fabio Fosso and is used here under CC BY-SA 2.0.

14. The 1987 publicity photograph of Michael Spinks is in the public domain because it was first published in the United States between 1923 and 1977 without a copyright notice. Typically, publicity photographs are not copyrighted because of the way in which they are intended to be used.

15. The 1928 photograph of Margaret Murray is in the public domain because it was taken in the United Kingdom prior to January 1, 1946. The photographer is unknown.

16. The 1886 self-portrait of Alfred Stieglitz is in the public domain because its copyright has expired.

17. The 1793 painting "The Death of Marat" by Jacques-Louis David is in the public domain because its copyright has expired. The original is in the Royal Museums of Fine Arts of Belgium.

18. The 2008 photograph of George Steinbrenner was released into the public domain by its authors MLB and archive.org.

19. The photograph of Friday the 13th circled in a calendar was taken by W. J. Pilsak, and is used here under CC BY-SA 3.0.

20. The 1951 photograph of Princess Elizabeth is from the collection of the National Archives UK (Work 21/292). No known copyright restrictions exist according to the National Archives.

21. The drawing of St. Anthony of Padua is copyright by Groendaal, and is used here under CC BY-SA 4.0.

22. The 1917 poster for the 140th Flag Day is in the public domain because its copyright has expired.

23. The painting "July" is from the *Brevarium Grimani*, circa 1510, and is in the public domain because its copyright has expired.

24. The photograph of a ruby was released into the public domain by its creator.

25. The photograph of a water lily at Kew Gardens was taken by "Dinkum," who released it into the public domain under the CC0 1.0 dedication.

26. The 1821 painting "Study of an Elm Tree" by John Constable is in the public domain because its copyright has expired. The painting is in the collection of the Victoria & Albert Museum, London.

27. The 1896 drawing "July" by Eugène Grasset is in the public domain because its copyright has expired.

28. The celestial sphere is from *Scenography of the Ptolemaic Cosmography*, by Johannes van Loon, based on Andreas

Cellarius's *Harmonia Macrocosmica*, 1660. It is in the public domain because its copyright has expired.

29. The 1906 automobile calendar is by Edward Penfield, and is in the collection of the Library of Congress Prints and Photographs Division. It is in the public domain because its copyright has expired.

30. The 50-year perpetual calendar photograph is in the public domain.

31. The cartoon by John T. McCutcheon is from his 1905 collection *The Mysterious Stranger and Other Cartoons* by John T. McCutcheon. It is in the public domain because its copyright has expired.

License Description and Terms

Aside from material purely in the public domain, photographs and other material in this book are used under specific licenses permitting free use, usually with an attribution requirement. For full text and terms of these licenses, click or enter the appropriate links below. If you believe there is an error in the copyright status or attribution of any of these images, please email us.

- Creative Commons Attribution 2.0 Generic (CC-BY 2.0): http://creativecommons.org/licenses/by/2.0/deed.en

- Creative Commons Attribution-Share Alike 3.0 Generic (CC-BY-SA 3.0): http://creativecommons.org/licenses/by-sa/3.0/

- Creative Commons Attribution-Share Alike 2.5 Generic (CC-BY-SA 2.5): http://creativecommons.org/licenses/by-sa/2.5/deed.en

- Creative Commons Attribution-Share Alike 2.0 Generic (CC-BY-SA 2.0): http://creativecommons.org/licenses/by/2.0/deed.en

- Creative Commons Attribution-Share Alike 1.0 Generic (CC-BY-SA 1.0): http://creativecommons.org/licenses/by-sa/1.0/deed.en

Timespinner
Press

Other Books from Timespinner Press

The Story of a Special Day
Michael Dobson

A series of (eventually) 366 volumes covering everything that happened on your special day! Events, births, deaths, quotes, holidays, and much more. It's like a birthday card they'll never throw away!

US$7.95 print / US$2.99 ebook.

From Plassey to Pakistan
Humayun Mirza

The history of British Colonial India and the formation of Pakistan from the unique perspective of the son of Pakistan's first president and last of the royal line of Bengal, Bihar, and Orissa! This unique historical document tells the inside story of this distinguished family, including the detailed story of the coup that toppled his father from power!

US$27.95 print

A Whole New Navy: America's War in the Pacific

Miles Durr

The most comprehensive and detailed description of America's naval war in the Pacific ever—every battle, every ship, every task force and every task group from Pearl Harbor through the Japanese surrender! A must-have for the collection of every World War II buff!

US$29.95 print

Improbable History: The Weird, the Obscure, and the Strangely Important

edited by Michael Dobson

From the birth of Western civilization to the rescue of Apollo 13, from the Leaning Tower of Pisa to Florence's Duomo, history has often turned on small, improbable details. Whatever happened to the ancient Samaritan people? Why did a fortuitous rainstorm allow the British to conquer India? How did an air raid in Italy lead to the development of chemotherapy? What happened when Albert Einstein met Adolf Hitler on the streets of Berlin? How did the Japanese manage to attack the US mainland using balloons? A cast of award-winning writers tackle some of the strangest tales in history!

US$19.95 print